FROM STONES
TO SKYSCRAPERS

DODD, MEAD & COMPANY · NEW YORK

FROM STONES
TO SKYSCRAPERS

A BOOK ABOUT ARCHITECTURE

By Thea and Richard Bergere

TO

JAD

Introduction

Almost everywhere we go there are buildings. We live, work, play, and pray in buildings. Some are simple; others are complicated or highly decorated structures. Some are very old; others are modern and new. The kind of building is determined by the place and the people who build it. It depends on what is needed and wanted, what materials are available to use.

Most living creatures know how to build. Insects, animals, and birds build nests, burrows or shelters for homes. But architecture is more than just an ability to build. Man alone has developed his building as an art. Like music, painting or sculpture, architecture is a *creative* process involving both skill and a love of beauty.

Man's first efforts to build were simple, but as civilization progressed, so did architecture. Over the centuries, styles of architecture and ways of building developed many variations and refinements in form and decoration. Building methods also changed, yet basic ideas first devised thousands of years ago are still used in modern construction. Influenced by climate, natural resources, religion, and the ways of living of different peoples, those primitive beginnings grew into the styles we know today.

5

Prehistoric

Prehistoric man of the Stone Age first sought shelter in caves. The struggle to survive, find food and defend himself was hard, and thousands of years passed before early man left his cave and attempted to build a dwelling with his roughly-fashioned stone tools. Materials were put together crudely but, nevertheless, it was the beginning of architecture.

The *post-and-lintel* system of construction was devised by primitive man when he discovered that two upright stones or posts would support a horizontal one. The post-and-lintel method is a basic structural principle in most buildings today, for straight walls, like posts, hold up the horizontal beams of floors and roofs.

The famous grouping of upright stones called Stonehenge, on the Salisbury Plain in England, represents the prehistoric form of post-and-lintel construction.

6

Stonehenge, England

After man learned to till the soil, he found it convenient to stay near his plot of land. A suitable cave might not be available nearby, but he could take shelter under trees and make a rude hut for himself by lashing overhead branches together and filling the spaces between the tree trunks with twigs and mud.

As a shepherd following his flocks, he needed a portable lodge, and found that animal hides could be wrapped around a frame of poles arranged in the form of of a cone. This tent was much like the tepee of the American Indian.

The stone cave gave primitive man the idea of building a stone hut. One type was built of flat stones placed in circular rows, with each row set inwards slightly more than the one below it. The resulting shape gave it the name, "beehive hut."

The post-and-lintel system was used in building a rectangular timber hut. Its walls were constructed of posts set into the ground apart from each other, connected at the top by horizontal beams. The spaces of this framework were closed with mud plastered over twigs and vines or, in mild climates, woven matting stretched between. Horizontal beams supported the flat roof of reeds and clay.

Thus, primitive man worked out the beginnings of architecture in fulfilling his need for shelter. The knowledge he gained is knowledge that is used in building today.

Twig hut

Tent

Beehive hut

Post-and-lintel timber hut

7

Egypt

As the Stone Age in Europe was coming to an end, about B. C. 2,000, men in other parts of the world had already progressed far beyond the simple tepee or hut. Egypt was already an advanced civilization.

The Great Sphinx, the pyramids, temples, obelisks — these symbolize Egypt to us. Thousands of years have gone by since Egyptian workers erected their massive stone structures, but their architecture remains and the skill that produced it is marveled at even today.

The river Nile was the center of civilization in Egypt. Its yearly overflow enriched the soil so that green fields were abundant with crops and palms. Bordering the river valley on both sides, steep cliffs provided limestone, sandstone and granite — materials that enabled the Egyptians to build their lasting monuments. The hard quality of these stones gave permanence to the pyramids and temples, now centuries old.

With almost no timber available, the Egyptians worked with stone, cutting and fitting it so accurately and so perfectly that even without mortar, walls remained solid and secure. Working out the use of the right angle in their building, a basic principle in architecture today, they achieved an amazing trueness in their calculations.

Climate influences the type of buildings constructed, and Egypt's climate, always clear and warm, also aided in their preservation. The extremely bright sunshine led to designs of great simplicity. Windows were little used, for roof slits and doors let enough light into the interiors. Thick, solid walls with few openings gave protection from the intense heat.

Building was done during the time of the annual flood, from July to October, when gardening was impossible and all of the people were available to work in the quarries, help transport the huge stones on rafts down the Nile, and finally, raise them into place.

Religion dominated the life of Egyptians. Believing that all things — living or inanimate — had a spirit, and that preservation of the body insured a life in the spirit world after death, they built structures to protect their dead. Temples and tombs were very important; they built them to last.

Portrait statues of the Pharaohs were common, for they insured the kings a continuing life in the spirit world if their mummified bodies should ever be destroyed. These were sometimes carved with the head of a Pharaoh on the body of a lion, the symbol of royal power. Such was the Great Sphinx at Gizeh, one of the Seven Wonders of the World. Built during the reign of Pharaoh Cheops (B. C. 3733), this unique monument is 66 feet high, 172 feet long, and its face alone is over 13 feet wide.

Great Sphinx at Gizeh

1

2

3

4

5

*Stone blocks
raised by the
wedge system*

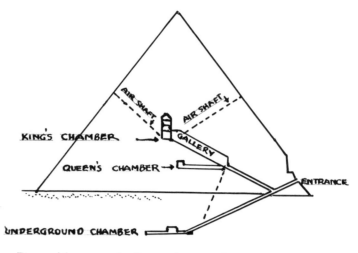

KING'S CHAMBER

QUEEN'S CHAMBER

AIR SHAFT

AIR SHAFT

GALLERY

ENTRANCE

UNDERGROUND CHAMBER

Pyramids were built to house the bodies of the Pharaohs, or kings. One of the largest and best known of the pyramid tombs is the Great Pyramid of Cheops at Gizeh. The base is about 755 feet square, covering nearly 13 acres. Its tip was 482 feet above the base, and except for the burial chambers within and the passages leading to them, the pyramid is solid stone. About 2,300,000 blocks of sandstone, many measuring 20 feet by 6 feet and weighing on an average of 5,000 pounds each, were fitted so perfectly to each other that no mortar was necessary. How they were lifted into place is not certain, but it is reasonable to suppose that it was done with the use of rockers and wedges — tapered blocks of wood pushed one at a time under the curved bottom of the rocker supporting the huge stone to be raised. It was slow though effective work. The labor of 100,000 men was required over a period of 20 years to complete this great pyramid.

Originally the pyramid was covered with a sloping smooth surface of fine white limestone, the joinings so exact that they were almost invisible. But in time, these casing stones were taken, piece by piece, by the builders of the city of Cairo. It was easier to appropriate them than to quarry their own stones from the cliffs.

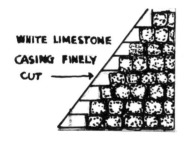

WHITE LIMESTONE
CASING FINELY
CUT →

Temples were built by the Pharaohs as pledges of devotion and offerings to the gods. These awe-inspiring monuments indicate the dominance and power of the priesthood and royalty, for they were not places of worship for the common people. Only the Pharaohs and priests were allowed inside to take part in mysterious rites. High enclosing walls hid the inner courts and halls from public view.

Luxor was one of the most famous temples. Occupying an area 1,200 feet by 360 feet, it was a *pylon-type* temple. Two massive gateway towers, called the *pylon,* formed the entrance. Approached through a broad avenue of sphinxes (A) and fronted by two *obelisks* (B), the pylon (C)

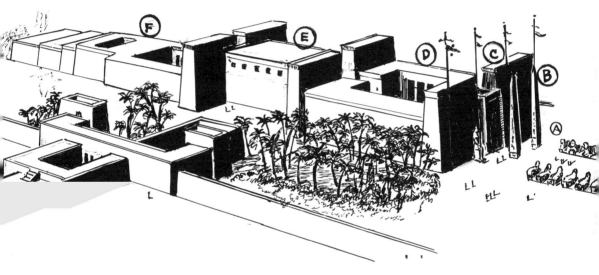

Temple of Luxor

was flat on top with sloping walls in pyramidal form. The outer court (D), with a colonnade on three sides, had no roof. The *hypostyle hall* (E) — a hall whose roof rests upon rows of columns — was restricted to the Pharaohs and priests, as was the sanctuary (F).

Sloping wall exteriors, one of the main characteristics of Egyptian architecture, were derived from the shape of the pyramids, which were known to resist the tremors of earthquakes.

Low relief

PALM

LOTUS

PAPYRUS

Broad expanses of wall space provided large areas for shallow carvings, called *low reliefs,* that were cut into the stone to record historical events on the outer walls of temples. Similar carvings on the interior walls were of a religious nature.

Hieroglyphics, the picture writing that used symbols for words and ideas, were added to the wall decorations to further complete the record-keeping. The Egyptians painted these carvings in brilliant reds, yellows and blues.

In this sunny land there was no problem of roof drainage. All roofs were flat, of stone slabs that helped keep out the heat. Priests used temple roofs for their processions, while the common people used the roofs of their houses as a place where they could enjoy the cool evening breezes.

The great weight of the stone roofs required many sturdy interior columns for support. The tops of the columns, known as the *capitals,* were in the shapes of familiar objects: the lotus blossom and bud (emblem of Upper Egypt), the papyrus flower (emblem of Lower Egypt), and the palm leaf which was used throughout the country.

The column shafts were circular, curving inwards toward the bottom, and were often representations in stone of the lotus or papyrus stalks tied together at intervals with carved crosswise bands. The columns sometimes stood on thick, unmolded bases.

12

Temple of Karnak

The Great Hypostyle Hall of Karnak had 134 columns in 16 rows, supporting the flat, massive stone roof which was of two levels. The center section was higher than the sides, and perforated stone slabs supporting this upper level formed what was called a "clear-story" and allowed light to enter. The taller central rows of columns, 80 feet high, had lotus flower capitals. The shorter side columns had capitals of the lotus bud.

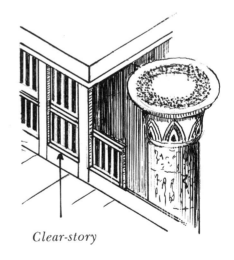

Clear-story

13

Obelisk

Each temple was dignified by a pair of obelisks at its entrance, varying in height from 70 to 105 feet. These were colossal *monoliths* — single blocks of granite — cut into four-sided tapering pillars with pyramid-shaped tops, and were covered with picture-writing hieroglyphics that recorded the triumphs and achievements of Pharaohs. To quarry, transport, and place one of these tremendous stones on its foundation was a remarkable feat of engineering, for the largest Egyptian obelisk in existence, now standing in the Piazza of St. John Lateran in Rome, weighs about 450 tons.

Theft and plundering of the pyramids caused later Pharaohs to carve out their tombs in the more protected area of the stone cliffs, and the Valley of the Tombs of the Kings was created.

The Great Temple at Abu Simbel is one of the most amazing of these rock-hewn tombs. Its entrance fore-court leads to a huge pylon-shaped structure 119 feet wide and 100 feet high, with four gigantic statues of Rameses II, all over 65 feet high.

Dêr-el-Bahari, built by Queen Hatshepsu, is considered the noblest of the tombs built against the sheer stone cliffs. The three vast terraces are open colonnaded courts that are connected to each other by broad sloping ramps. The top terrace, with a sacrificial hall and ancient altar, leads to the sanctuary carved deep into the limestone rock.

14

Abu Simbel

Dêr-el-Bahari

Hanging Gardens of Babylon

Babylonia

The kind of buildings, the style of architecture, in any land reflects the way of life of the people — what they believed in, and what sort of climate they lived in, their traditions and culture.

Almost as old as Egyptian civilization was that of Babylonia in Asia Minor. Over 4,000 years ago the fabulous city of Babylon was noted for its "Hanging Gardens," another of the Seven Wonders of the World. They were not "hanging" in our sense of the word, but were planted on an artificial terraced hill about 75 feet high and 900 feet square at its base. Built and tended by the slaves of King Nebuchadnezzar, this lush foliaged, flowering structure was a strikingly beautiful landmark on the flat, treeless plains along the Euphrates river.

There are no lasting monuments of Babylonia as there are of Egyptian architecture. There was no stone or timber in the area with which to build them — only an abundance of clay deposited on the banks of the river. But the resourceful Babylonians compressed the clay in molds, dried it in the sun, and made bricks which became their chief building material.

Babylonia was a fertile country; the people prospered as farmers and traders. But much of the region was swampland where rain fell heavily for weeks on end. During the long summers, swarms of insects plagued the populace and the Babylonians learned to erect their buildings upon huge, brick platforms 30 to 50 feet above the plain to avoid them.

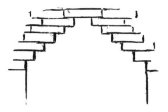

Corbeled arch

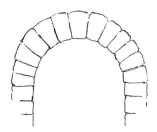

Round Arch

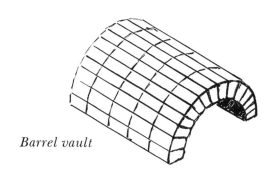

Barrel vault

Dome, Babylonian

The sun-dried bricks made by the Babylonians were about 15 inches square and from two to four inches thick. They were used for the building platforms and as the central portions of walls, to which a facing of colored glazed brick was added.

Use of bricks led to the development of the *arch* and *dome* — major steps forward in the story of architecture. Post-and-lintel construction as used by the Egyptians was not practical in Babylonia; it required horizontal beams large enough to span wide openings and there were none to be had. Arches, the most important feature in Babylonian architecture, were first formed by *corbeling;* that is, each horizontal row of bricks projected slightly beyond the one below it, so that the width of the opening to be covered was lessened row by row until it was closed over at the top. Later, true arches were constructed with radiating *voussoirs* — wedge-shaped bricks. This type of arch, when extended in depth to cover over the entire length of a walled passage, became known as a *barrel vault*.

The Babylonians successfully created a dome with bricks, using the same method of corbeling they had learned in forming arches.

Bitumen, a tar-like substance which came from springs along the river, was used for cementing bricks together and waterproofing roofs.

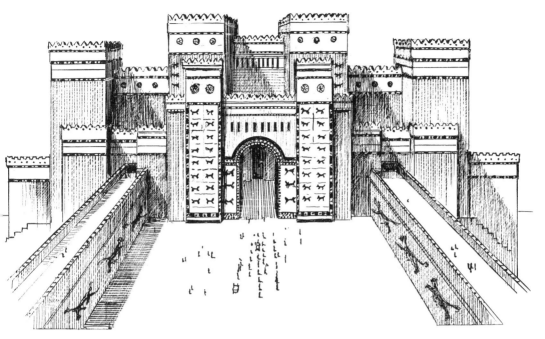

Ishtar Gate

The city of Babylon was surrounded by an immense city wall of bricks that was so broad a four-horse chariot could turn around on top of it. The wall had 100 bronze gates, but the main entrance to the city was the Ishtar Gate that was 40 feet high and had six tall towers. It was ornamented with designs of animals which were molded of clay and glazed in brilliant colors of red, white and yellow. The avenue leading to the gate was lined with high walls covered with colored glazed brick depicting a procession of roaring lions. The tops of all walls, towers, and buildings in Babylon were finished with battlemented cresting.

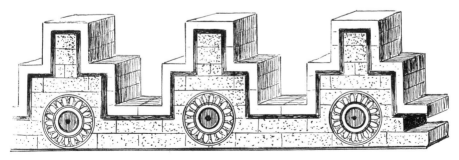

Battlemented cresting

A superstitious people, there were great figures of man-headed bulls to guard palace entrances against evil spirits. Life after death did not concern the Babylonians as it did the Egyptians, and so they were not tomb-builders. Rather, they worshipped the stars, the planets, and their many gods. The priests, holding great power over the people, were astrologers who foretold the future by the stars and interpreted the will of the gods from temple observatories atop high *ziggurats*.

Ziggurats, meaning holy mountains, were pyramid-like buildings that towered up in diminishing terraces, round which an inclined ramp led to the top where there was an elaborately decorated sanctuary.

The Ziggurat in Babylon was 272 feet square, 160 feet high, and was topped with a shrine to Nebo, god of wisdom and agriculture. A record found in the crumbled ruins states that it had seven receding stories, dedicated to the seven heavenly planets, each one faced with a different color of glazed brick.

The clay of which the city was built, not as enduring as the stone of Egypt and later civilizations, could not withstand the effects of wars, fires and the weathering of centuries. All that exists of Babylon today is ruins.

Ziggurat of Babylon

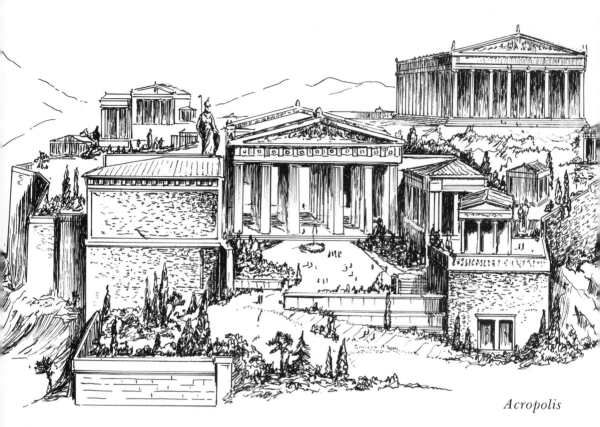

Acropolis

Greece

High on a hill, overlooking and dominating the city of Athens, is the world-famous Acropolis. Its buildings are now mere fragments of their original beauty, but the loveliest of all Greek temples, the Parthenon, crowns its top.

Architecture reached a peak of perfection in the hands of Greek craftsmen of both artistic and mathematical ability. The Grecian style that is recognized today influenced architecture in almost every country in Western civilization, but its particular beauty has never been equalled.

The most important buildings were the temples, differing greatly from those of Egypt or Babylonia because the religion of Greece differed greatly. Here there were no powerful priests; both men and women participated in celebrations to gods and goddesses. Governed democratically, the Greeks were intellectual, loved beauty, liked sports and found great joy in living.

22

Greek temples were public buildings. Relatively small, they were intended only to house a statue of the god or goddess to whom the temple was dedicated, and sometimes a treasury. Religious ceremonies were held outdoors in the clear, crystalline atmosphere of the country, and so emphasis was placed on exterior beauty of the buildings for all the people to enjoy.

The usual temple was small, oblong, and built upon a low stepped platform with columns on four sides and a sloping roof to shed the rain. The roof projected from the ends to form *porticoes,* or porches, where people could take shelter from sudden showers. The triangular-shaped wall section over the porticoes, called the *pediment,* was often decorated with sculpture.

Wood hut to small temples

Greek architecture developed the post-and-lintel sytsem to its highest standards. This method of building, used by the Egyptians, is generally considered to have been an outgrowth of the wood hut with upright posts devised by primitives.

A wealth of marble, the ideal building stone, was to be found in the mountains of Greece, and was particularly abundant in Mount Pentelicon near Athens. Hard enough to weather well in Greece's moderate climate, and fine-grained so that it could be easily cut, shaped, and carved into the most delicate and precise forms, this stone was wonderful material for the craftsmen to work with. Gradually they designed and perfected three "Orders of Architecture" known as the Doric, Ionic, and Corinthian. An *order* is the term given to a column and the horizontal lintel beams it supports.

Metopes and triglyphs

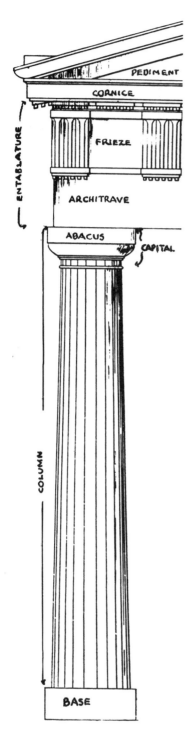

Doric Order

The Doric Order expresses sturdiness and strength. It developed with the first Greek temples, perhaps as early as B. C. 800, and was slowly refined into its final form as seen in the Parthenon.

The column stands without a base, directly on the temple platform. Its circular shaft is carved into 20 shallow grooves called *flutes,* which meet in sharp edges. The shaft itself has a slight swelling called an *entasis,* for straight-sided columns give the optical illusion of bending inwards. The *capital* has three to five narrow horizontal bands from which curves a bowl-shaped molding, topped by a square *abacus.*

An order consists of a column and the horizontal portion it supports. The technical term for the horizontal section is *entablature,* and it consists of the *architrave, frieze* and *cornice.*

In the Doric Order, the architrave is plain. The frieze has squares called *metopes,* alternating with *triglyphs* which are blocks having three vertical channels. Sometimes, as in the Parthenon, the metopes are ornamented with sculpture. The cornice is the crowning and slightly projecting part of the entablature.

Parthenon

The Parthenon (B. C. 447-432) is the outstanding building on the Acropolis of Athens. Designed by Ictinus and Callicrates, this temple, dedicated to Athena Parthenos, the patron goddess of Athens, is the best example of the Doric Order. It was 228 feet long, 101 feet wide, and had 46 columns ranging its exterior. The columns, 34 feet tall, supported an entablature 11 feet high.

Pheidias, the master sculptor of the time, decorated the square metopes of the frieze with a sculptured procession depicting the festival of Athens. He filled the triangular-shaped areas of the pediments with over-sized figures of Olympian gods. He also created a wondrous statue of ivory and gold, 40 feet tall, representing Athena, that stood in the "naos" or statue chamber of the Parthenon.

Upper parts of temples were painted in red and blue, with small touches of green, black, yellow and gold. The frieze of the Parthenon had additional bronze trimming of wreathes, swords and shields attached to the figures, which are thought to have been a gift from Alexander the Great in B. C. 334.

The Parthenon as it appears

As it was built

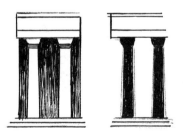

As it would appear without refinements

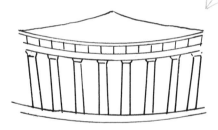

Light columns against dark background seem heavier than dark columns against light area, yet all are the same size.

Perfection of line was the goal of the Greek architects, for they wanted their temples to have grace, solidity, fine proportions, and to appear beautiful from every angle. Since the eye often deceives, creating optical illusions, they curved the major lines of buildings in the opposite direction to which they would appear to the viewer.

Long horizontal lines, for instance, when seen from below, seem to sag in the middle. Ictinus and Callicrates allowed for this defect in human vision by slightly raising the platform and entablature of the Parthenon almost three inches in the center of the porticoes, and four-and-one-half inches at the centers of the sides. Columns, with their slight swelling of the shaft, were slanted inwards a little toward the top, so that they would not look as if they were leaning forward. Those at the corners were spaced closer together to give the effect of greater strength, and they were heavier than the others because the brightness of the sky made them appear thinner.

There are no perfectly straight lines in the whole of the Parthenon, but the *refinements,* as these adjustments are called, were so carefully worked out that it was only in recent years that scholars discovered the fact that they existed.

Shattered by a shell in 1687, the partially restored ruins of the Parthenon still show much of its original grace.

26

Temple of Diana

The second Greek order of architecture is the Ionic. Its capital is noted for the pair of graceful spirals, called *volutes* or scrolls, which may have been derived from the nautilus shell.

Columns were not a single piece of marble, but were formed of sections called *drums,* held together by wood and metal *dowels,* or pins. Only the top and bottom parts had the flutes carved on them before being placed into position. The others were finished later, to insure precise alignment of the grooves.

The Temple of Artemis (Diana), at Ephesus in Asia Minor (B.C. 356), was one of the most impressive Ionic temples. Considered one of the Seven Wonders of the World, it was noted for the sculptured pedestals and drums of its front columns, designed by Scopas, a master sculptor.

27

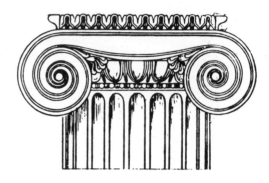

Ionic capital

Corinthian capital

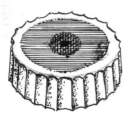

*Column section
showing dowel*

The column of the Ionic Order, distinguished by the decorative spiral scrolls of its capital, is more slender than that of the Doric Order. It has 24 deep flutes that are separated by narrow flat bands instead of sharp edges, and it also has a deeply molded base.

The lightest and most ornate of the three Greek orders of architecture is the Corinthian. Its bell-shaped capital, covered with *acanthus* leaves, later became a favorite with the Romans.

The Mausoleum at Halicarnassos (B. C. 353) was the tomb of King Mausolos, and was another of the Seven Wonders of the World. The tomb chamber, surrounded by Ionic columns, was raised on a square foundation. It was covered with a pyramid-shaped roof that was topped with a grouping of horses, a chariot and riders, sculptured of marble.

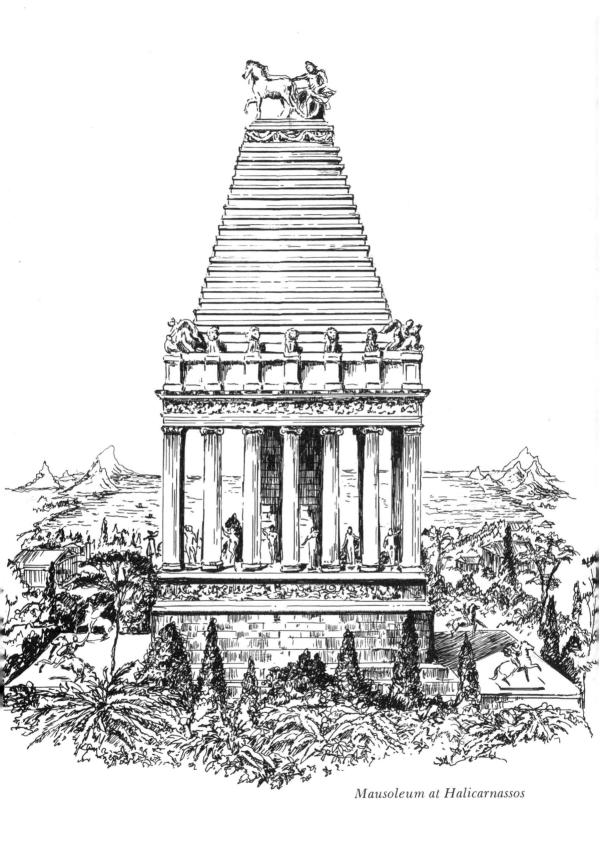

Mausoleum at Halicarnassos

Porch of the Maidens

The Erechtheion (B. C. 420-393) is an Ionic temple built on the Acropolis near the Parthenon. This view is of the south portico, sometimes called the "Porch of the Maidens" because of the draped female figures that take the place of columns supporting the entablature.

30

Choragic Monument

The Choragic Monument in
Athens (B. C. 335) was built to
uphold a trophy won by Lysicrates
and his company in competition at
a Grecian dance festival. The six
columns of the Corinthian order
are joined to a circular marble
structure that stands upon a square
stone base. The plume-like decoration on top held the award.

Of many monuments erected to
honor athletes and musicians, this
is the only one remaining.

31

Rome

The view of Imperial Rome, above, has long since been changed; only fragments of the ancient past remain scattered throughout the city. The Romans were excellent builders who had enduring materials to use, and their structures would have lasted through the centuries until today had it not been for deliberate destruction. Emperors often tore down noteworthy buildings built by previous rulers to make room for bigger, more impressive structures. The advance of Christianity took its toll, too. Temples representing the Pagan religion were dismantled and ruined.

Modern building owes a great deal to the Roman developments in

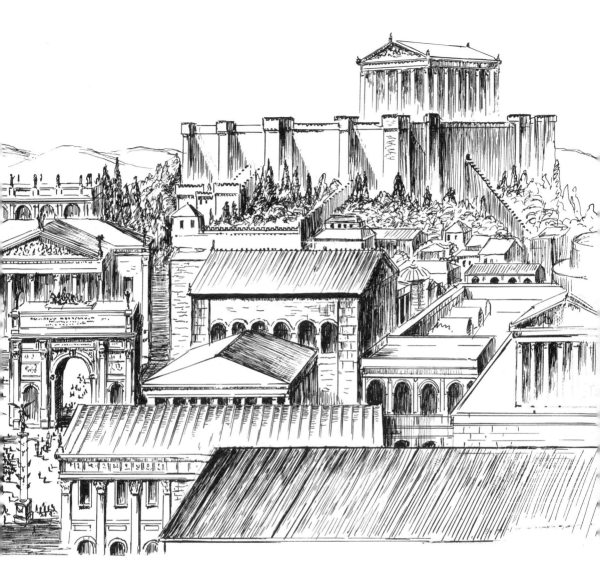

architecture. One of Rome's great contributions was the use of concrete in construction, a basic material used today. Concrete removed the limitations of the Greek method of building. The Greeks were precise in grinding the surfaces of marble blocks so that they fitted together perfectly, needing only metal clamps to secure them, but that took time and craftsmanship and also restricted the size of the buildings. Concrete enabled the Romans to construct buildings of vast dimensions never before achieved. It allowed the employment of much unskilled labor, and it could be made in any country regardless of natural resources available. Roman architecture spread throughout the Empire which, by the year A. D. 50, included Europe, North Africa and western Asia.

33

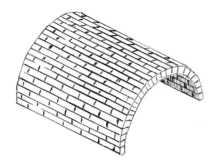

Barrel vault, Roman

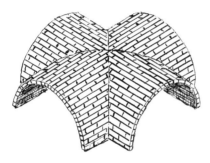

Cross vault

Dome, Roman

The arch, vault and dome are prominent features of Roman architecture. Though they were created by much earlier peoples, concrete was the important material that helped to further their development. The Romans could cast them in one piece — stronger, higher, and bigger than ever before.

Some vaults were constructed so large that they were never equalled in size until steel was introduced for building at the end of the 19th century. The *barrel vault,* formerly a simple arched covering for only a narrow rectangular room, grew to span a width of 100 feet. Then the Romans invented the *cross vault* by cutting through one barrel vault with another, which enabled them to roof over square apartments. Circular buildings were designed with great round domes, and more complex structures were created with the addition of semi-domes.

All these forms of cast concrete, once set and hardened into rigid masses of stone, were sturdy and solid. There was little or no outward pressure, and the concrete walls, usually faced with brick or marble, gave enough support from below for the arches, vaults and domes they upheld. Columns were no longer necessary as they had been in the hypostyle halls of Egypt or in the Greek temples, although the Romans continued to use them on building exteriors for decoration.

The Romans adopted the Doric, Ionic, and Corinthian orders from the Greeks, and created two more — the Tuscan and Composite — making a total of five Orders of Architecture.

They slightly changed the Doric Order, making the column thinner with a molded base, and adding *dentils* — projecting tooth-like cubes — to the cornice.

The Tuscan Order, very much like the Doric, has a simple molded capital and a plain entablature, but is heavier and has an unfluted column. It was not decorative enough to suit the Roman taste and was not often used.

The Ionic Order was simplified in the Roman version with smaller, more geometric volutes on the capital. Later, *angle volutes* were used, such as those seen on the columns of the Temple of Saturn (page 38).

The Corinthian Order, a favorite with the Romans, was further elaborated with a scroll and leaf decoration on the frieze, and a series of bracket-shaped scrolls on the lower part of the cornice.

The capital of the Composite Order has two rows of acanthus leaves, with a double volute, and is really an ornate combination of the Corinthian and Ionic designs. It was mainly used on triumphal arches for its elaborate ornamentation.

Orders were frequently superimposed; that is, placed one above another, as in the Colosseum (page 39), and also placed on pedestals to increase their height.

Angle volute

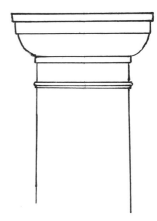

Tuscan capital

Composite capital

35

Pantheon, Rome

The Roman religion was similar to that of the Greeks. They worshipped a variety of gods and goddesses, many of them the same as the Greek ones but known under Latin names. Lacking the enthusiasm of the Greeks, however, they did not build as many temples. As the wealth, position and influence of the city grew, the Romans desired public buildings, palaces and monuments in the form of arches or columns. They were excellent road and bridge builders and, conscious of the need for adequate water supply, they also built the famous aqueducts.

The Pantheon in Rome (A. D. 124), an imposing circular structure built by Emperor Hadrian, is in the best condition of all the ancient Roman buildings. Dedicated to all the gods, its dome, the largest of its kind at the time, has an interior height and diameter of 142 feet and was originally covered with gilded bronze plates. Its windowless walls of concrete 20 feet thick were once faced with gleaming white marble.

As shown in its original form on the opposite page, the pediment above the Corinthian-columned portico once had bronze sculpture which has since been removed. Yet, stripped of its trimmings, the Pantheon, at one time a pagan temple and used today as a Christian church, is still impressive.

The remains of the Temple of Saturn in Rome (A. D. 284), pictured on the following page, show columns of the Ionic Order. One of the oldest monuments in the Roman Forum, the eight Ionic columns date from a restoration in the fourth century. The ruins of the Forum, a public meeting place around which were grouped important public buildings, are situated in the heart of modern Rome.

The Pantheon today

Temple of Saturn

The Romans loved sports events and violent exhibitions of mortal combat. The gigantic Colosseum in Rome (A. D. 70-82) could hold 50,000 spectators and for over 300 years it was a place of brutality. There were fights between gladiators, battles of men against wild beasts, and fights to the finish by natural enemies of the animal kingdom. Blood that fell was absorbed by the sand spread for that purpose, and the open area came to be called the *arena*, the Latin word for sand or beach.

The Colosseum was the greatest of the amphitheaters, with an arena measuring 287 feet by 180 feet. The exterior was four stories high, the top one an almost unbroken wall. The others were designed with a series of arches, 80 in each story, which were set on *piers* with attached half columns. The Tuscan Order decorated the first or ground story, the Ionic was used for the second story, and Corinthian columns appeared on the third. The flat, projecting, column-like *pilasters* on the top story were also of the Corinthian Order. The entire structure was of cement, faced with brick on the interior and *travertine,* the Roman limestone, on the exterior. The Colosseum was stupendous, and even now in its ruined condition, it is an imposing relic of the past.

Colosseum

Castel Sant' Angelo (Hadrian's Tomb)

The Emperior Hadrian designed and supervised the building of his
own tomb in Rome about the year 135 A. D. Now known as Castel Sant'
Angelo, its square base about 300 feet wide and 75 feet high was formerly
faced with white marble. The huge round tower, circled with columns,
was topped with a dome of marble, planted with oaks and evergreens.

The Romans created the triumphal arch to honor emperors or famous
men. The Arch of Titus in Rome (A. D. 81), built after the death of
Emperor Titus, was noted for its beautiful proportion and fine details
of carving.

40

Arch of Titus

Santa Sophia

Byzantine

Expanding trade routes soon linked the East of Persia and Egypt with the West of Rome and Europe, and architectural ideas — as well as other aspects of culture — spread and were interchanged.

Byzantium was made the capital of the Roman Empire in A. D. 330 and renamed Constantinople in honor of Emperor Constantine. The Emperor had accepted Christianity as the state religion of his Empire in A. D. 323 and the main buildings erected in the new capital were churches.

The architecture that developed was called Byzantine. With no good building stone available, but with a knowledge of making hard bricks, Byzantine builders combined the traditional domed style of the East, that had originated with the Babylonian users of bricks, and Roman construction methods of the West. The "onion-top" dome became a prominent feature. Most often it was used in groups to cover a single building. Varying in type, domes were placed over square structures, whereas the Romans earlier had only used them on circular ones.

Santa Sophia, built in Constantinople (now Istanbul in Turkey) in A. D. 532-537, is one of the most famous examples of Byzantine architecture.

Built of brick and concrete, the church outwardly gives little hint of the magnificent beauty of its interior.

Inside, the central dome measures 107 feet in diameter and rises 180 feet above the ground. It rests upon four semicircular arches called *pendentives,* which are supported by four massive stone *piers.*

The two lower half-domes, east and west, connect with the great arches and help buttress, or brace, the main dome. The huge vaulted space enclosed, unobstructed by columns, forms an oval 225 feet long by 107 feet wide. Rings of small arched windows, set into the bases of the domes, light the richly decorated interior.

Here, as in all Byzantine buildings, are *mosaics,* designs created by setting small bits of brilliantly colored glass into cement. In Santa Sophia the mosaics covering the vaults and domes represent angels, saints and apostles, but many were covered over with plaster when the the church became a Mohammedan *mosque* after the Turks captured Constantinople in 1453.

Delicate and intricate carving on railings, screens, pulpits and capitals are typical of Byzantine architecture. It was done by drilling away the background of the design, leaving the outer surface smooth and in its original outline.

Capitals were carved in a variety of lacy patterns. The bird-and-basket type was popular and is one of the most effective designs.

PENDETIVE

Interior, Santa Sophia

Bird-and-basket capital

43

Cathedral of San Marco

The Cathedral of San Marco (A. D. 1042-1065) is a Byzantine church in Venice, Italy, with five domes. Overlooking the famous Piazza di San Marco, its exterior glitters with an array of mosaic work. Interior walls are faced with colored marble, and over the surfaces of vaults and domes, mosaic pictures portray stories from the Bible.

44

Romanesque

The "Dark Ages" in Europe, marked by a decline of learning and the arts, followed the fall of the Roman Empire. Much of the building during this early medieval period was done by monks, and the style was sober and dignified. As the strength of the Christian church grew, a style of architecture known as Romanesque developed. Based on ancient Roman forms, it was characterized by rough stone exteriors, Roman methods of vaulting, and rounded arches set on pillar-like piers. Later, ornamentation was added.

Three famous Romanesque buildings stand together in Italy: the Pisa Cathedral, Baptistery, and Campanile, the latter readily recognized as the "Leaning Tower of Pisa."

Baptistery, Cathedral, Campanile at Pisa

Campaniles are bell-towers, standing separate from a church or cathedral. Used to call Christians to worship, they were adopted from the Mohammedan *minarets,* slender towers from which the faithful were called to prayer.

The round campanile of Pisa (A. D. 1174) is an architectural enigma, leaning 16 feet off-center. Its foundation began settling on one side as soon as the second story was finished. The builders could not correct the lean that resulted, and work was stopped after completion of the fourth story.

Sixty years later the lean had not increased, and three more stories were built, making the tower 151 feet tall. The top story, the belfry, was not added until A. D. 1350.

The ornamental bands of columns and arches encircling the tower are called *arcades.* The Pisa Cathedral (A. D. 1092) and the circular Baptistery (A. D. 1278) are also arcaded, a decorative feature frequently used in later Romanesque architecture.

The cathedral is noted for having introduced the "Latin cross" plan that later became common to most churches in western Europe. The cross is formed by the addition of two "arms" called *transepts* that extend at right angles from the sides of the church. The crossing where the transepts meet the *nave,* or main body of the church, has a dome. A timber roof covers the remainder.

Latin cross

46

Abbaye-aux-Hommes, Caen

Romanesque architecture was similar throughout western Europe. However, the low-sloped roofs and small windows of buildings in the south did not suit the duller climate of the north where large windows were necessary to let enough light into the interiors, and high-pitched roofs were needed to shed rain and snow. The Romanesque Abbaye-aux-Hommes at Caen in France (A. D. 1066-77) has a steep-sloped roof and many tall, round-arched windows in its otherwise plain exterior.

Ribbed vaulting, an advancement of the heavy Roman vault, enabled builders to construct very high, yet lightweight supporting vaults by means of a skeleton frame of arches that held thin panels of stone. Since these arches rested on slender supporting piers, walls could be thin, with numerous windows, because they were no longer used for major support.

47

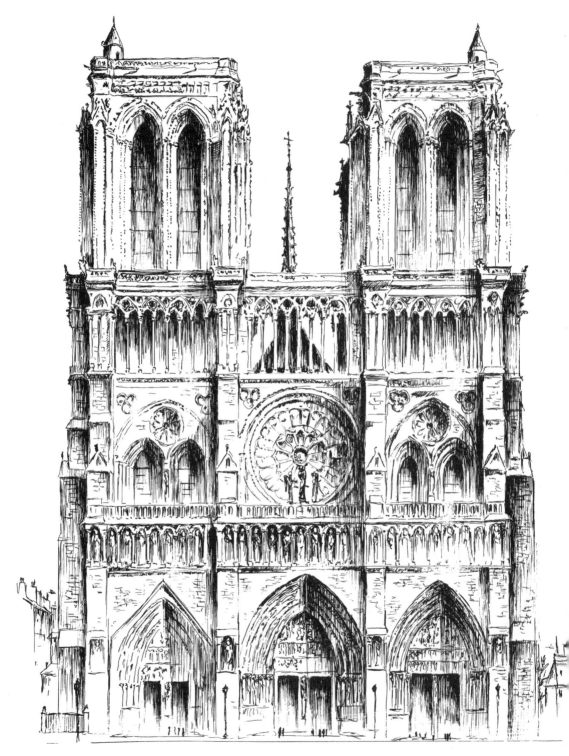

Notre Dame, Paris

Gothic

In the 13th century, the power of the church was immense. Religious enthusiasm was at its height throughout the kingdoms and nations of western Europe. Church ceremonies and rituals were elaborate, the number of clergy had increased, and multitudes of worshippers made pilgrimages to shrines and holy relics. Towns and cities competed in building impressive cathedrals.

Ribbed vaulting

Variations in Gothic architecture were caused by differences of climate and natural resources of the various countries of Europe, but the style was basically derived from the Romanesque period. Pointed arches, tapering spires and pinnacles are distinctive Gothic features. This vertical, aspiring effect was emphasized in the north by the high-pitched roofs and tall *traceried* windows of decorative, interlacing lines.

The use of ribbed vaulting and pointed arches enabled Gothic builders to create very high interior sections of churches or cathedrals. The vaulting was supported by huge piers inside and massive, projecting structures, called *buttresses,* which rose from the ground outside. From the tops of these buttresses sprang two half-arches, the *flying buttresses,* which rested against the main wall and aided in making the structure balanced and stable.

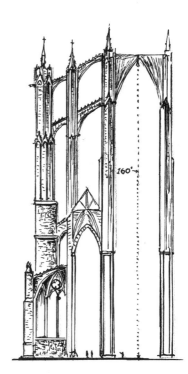

Flying buttress

49

Elongated figures, Chartres

Primarily, there were two kinds of Gothic ornament used — stained glass windows and sculpture.

Stained glass windows decorated the interiors of the cathedrals and gave light that was needed in the dark climate of the north. But more important than that, their religious scenes served to illustrate the story of the Bible for the people, most of whom could not read.

Decorative openwork in stone, called *tracery,* formed the ornamental patterns in circular rose windows. Tracery also filled the upper parts of the tall windows, crowning the glowing stained glass pictures beneath. In "plate" tracery, the design was cut through a flat plate of stone. Later, more intricate designs were made possible with "bar" tracery in which stone bars were fitted together.

Sculpture in the form of elongated figures, with drapery lines mainly vertical so that they gave a column-like effect, adorned the doorways. They were carved from simple building stone. Gargoyles were water spouts carved in grotesque forms. They projected from the upper part of a building, usually from the roof gutter.

Gothic architecture in its purest form can be found in France, where the style started a half-century earlier than in England. Notre Dame in Paris (A.D. 1163-1235) is one of the oldest of French Gothic cathedrals, an excellent example of the northern style.

Gargoyle, Paris

Rose window

Although Notre Dame is incomplete, since its towers were never carried up to their intended height, the impressive western *facade,* as shown on page 52, has been copied for many later churches. Three deeply recessed doorways, each one a different design, shelter numerous statues of saints, and above, statues of the kings of France are banded in a row. The magnificent rose window is 42 feet in diameter. An arcaded screen across the top of the facade connects the two towers.

The slim, graceful, flying buttresses of the east end, shown in the illustration on the following page, give it a delicate appearance.

51

Notre Dame, showing flying buttresses

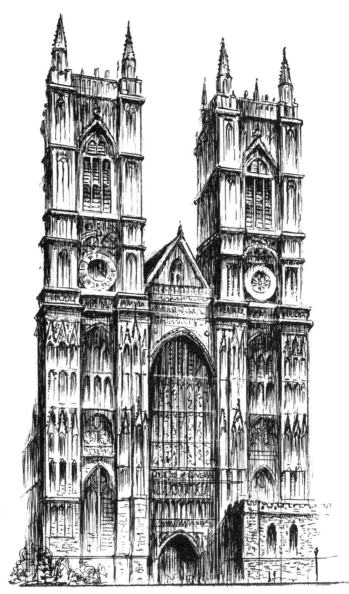

Westminster Abbey

Westminster Abbey, England's most famous Gothic building, was originally a Benedictine monastery founded in A. D. 960. Other notable examples of Gothic architecture shown on the following pages are: Antwerp Cathedral, the most impressive church in Belgium; Cologne Cathedral, the largest Gothic church in northern Europe; Chateau de Pierrefonds, typical of many castles built during the 13th and 14th centuries; and the Palazzo Cavalli, a Gothic palace on the Grand Canal in Venice.

53

Antwerp Cathedral

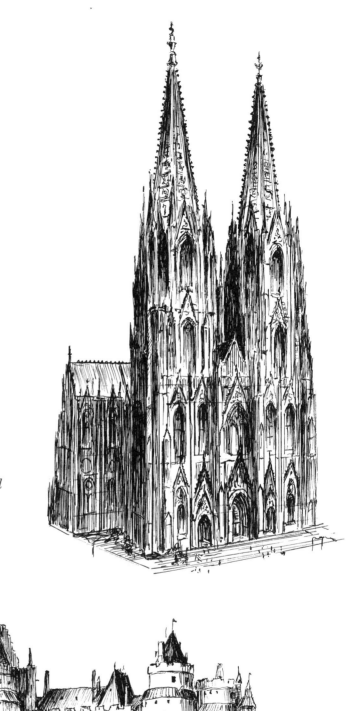

Cologne Cathedral

Chateau Pierrefonds

Palazzo Cavalli, Venice

Renaissance

The word *renaissance* means a revival or new birth. The Renaissance movement of the 15th and 16th centuries was a revival of the Roman style and the five Orders of Architecture. It started, quite naturally, in Italy, spreading later all over western Europe. Architects found inspiration in the ruins of ancient Roman monuments and, concentrating on beauty of design, adapted the older style to suit the requirements of the new buildings.

It took 120 years to build St. Peter's Cathedral in Rome (A. D. 1506-1626), which is the largest church in the world and the climax building of the Renaissance. It stands in majestic splendor overlooking the great colonnade-encircled entrance court, the Piazza San Pietro, with its twin fountains and central obelisk. Corinthian columns and *pilasters* over 90 feet tall grace the portico which is 234 feet wide.

The plan of St. Peter's forms a Latin cross, 600 feet long and 450 feet across the transepts, or arms. The crossing is covered by a huge dome that has an internal diameter of over 137 feet. Four massive piers, 60 feet square, support this great dome of brickwork, and ten chains are placed within its base at intervals to prevent it from spreading.

The dome of St. Peter's, with its crowning *lantern*, soars 452 feet above the ground, twice as tall as the towers of Westminster Abbey, and dominating all views of Rome.

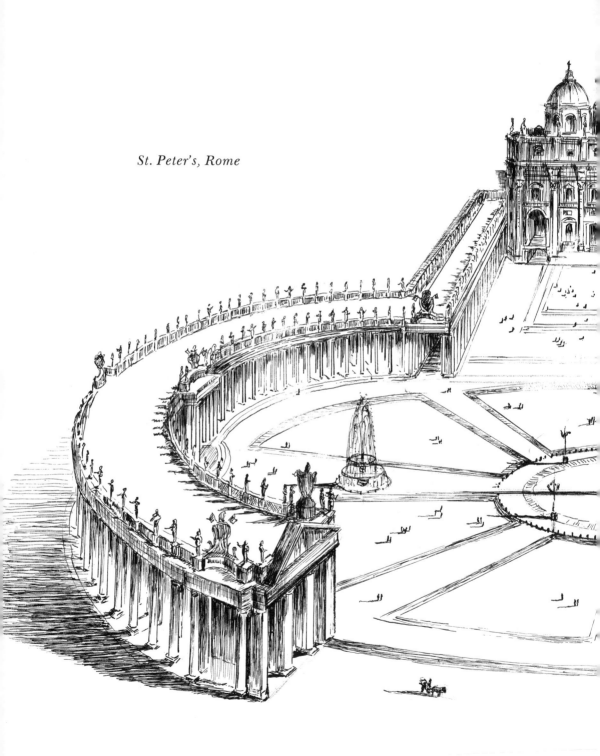

St. Peter's, Rome

St. Paul's, London

In England, Renaissance architecture was not quickly adopted, but after the Great Fire of London in 1666, many buildings and churches were erected in that style, including St. Paul's Cathedral (A. D. 1675-1710), designed by Sir Christopher Wren. Columns of the Corinthian and Composite orders are used on the facade. Like St. Peter's, it is of the Latin cross plan, with an interior length of 463 feet. The huge dome, 112 feet in diameter at its base, stands upon a high "drum" with an arrangement of columns circling it. Bold dignity characterizes St. Paul's, making this church a dominant structure in the heart of London.

The Library of San Marco in Venice (A. D. 1536) is in the later Renaissance style. Its columns of the Doric and Ionic Orders, with beautiful arches, are arranged like those of the Colosseum. The sculptured detail, although boldly carved to produce strong contrast of light and shadow, is refined and delicate.

60

Library of San Marco, Venice

Pantheon, Paris

For about fifty years after the Renaissance style appeared in France, buildings were still constructed in the native Gothic tradition, with only Renaissance details added to them. Later in the 17th century, the architecture developed into the true style.

The Pantheon in Paris (A. D. 1764-90), with Corinthian columns, is built on a Greek cross plan, having a square central area and four equal arms. Its windowless walls strikingly contrast with the classic portico.

Spanish architects, like the French, applied Renaissance details to Gothic buildings. The Santiago de Compostela Cathedral is a Gothic church, but its west facade, built in the Late Period of Renaissance (A. D. 1738), shows the ornate Renaissance styling known as Baroque.

62

Santiago de Compostela

Baroque

Baroque — a word meaning irregular in form, grotesque, fantastic — was a term given to a lavish style of architecture that appeared toward the end of the 17th century after the vigor of the true Renaissance had died down. Starting in Italy, then later spreading over western Europe, the style was, in a sense, a rebellion of the architects against the rules and regulations on plan, design, and ornament that governed the later period of Renaissance building.

Baroque style has often been described as the architecture of the curved line. Buildings are heavily decorated with huge, wavy scrolls, sculptured figures in fanciful flight, luxuriously detailed carved ornament, and columns with twisted shafts, all expressing the joyous independence of the architects.

Santa Maria della Salute in Venice (A. D. 1632) is a splendid example of Baroque architecture. The great dome with the high drum and scrolled buttresses is the outstanding feature of this octagonal building.

Santa Maria della Salute

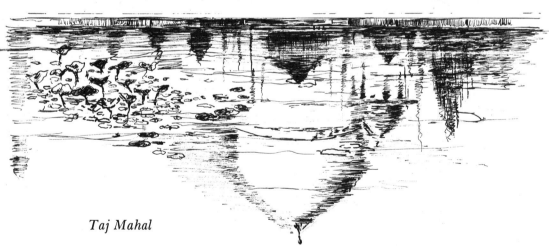

Taj Mahal

The Taj Mahal in India (A. D. 1630-45) is a magnificent white marble mausoleum built by Shah Jehan in memory of his favorite wife.

66

Saracenic

One of the most beautiful monuments in the world, the graceful design and rich, delicate ornamentation of the Taj Mahal make it one of the best examples of Saracenic architecture.

"Saracen" was a term originally applied to aggressive Arab tribes that roamed the Sahara Desert and troubled the borders of the Roman Empire. In the Middle Ages, Christians gave the name "Saracen" to Moslem followers of Mohammed (A. D. 570-632) and the architecture of the Moslems therefore came to be known as Saracenic. Their most important buildings were mosques and tombs.

Characteristics of the style vary, for the Moslems invaded many countries and in each adopted whatever type of architecture they found. Yet certain features are typical, especially the bulb-shaped domes and graceful minarets.

Interior walls are richly decorated with floral and geometric patterns of interlacing lines. The intricate designs are called *arabesques,* and are usually done in colorful tile mosaics.

Windows, kept small because of the heat, have lacelike screens of thin, pierced marble. Arches are of four kinds. Horseshoe and scalloped arches appeared in Spain and North Africa. The *ogee,* or keel arch, was employed in Persia and India. The pointed arch, a symbol of faith, was used in all these countries.

67

Alhambra, Granada

Pierced marble window

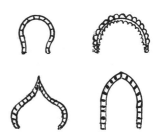

Arches: horseshoe, scalloped ogee, pointed

The Giralda in Spain (A. D. 1159) is a notable example of Saracenic architecture and one of the most beautiful towers in the world. It is 45 feet square and 185 feet high, and is decorated with long panels of a geometric pattern. The belfry with its colossal bronze statue of Faith was added in A. D. 1568.

Giralda, Seville

68

St. Basil's, Moscow

Rusian architecture up to the 15th century was true Byzantine, influenced by Constantinople and the Greek Orthodox Church. The onion-shaped dome, in a variety of sizes, designs and colors, became a picturesque characteristic of Russian buildings about the 16th century. St. Basil's Church (A.D. 1555) in Moscow typifies this domed style.

Great Temple at Madura

The Hindu architecture of India is characterized mainly by its lavish stone sculpture. Elaborate carving appears on all surfaces of the stately temples, which are colossal in size and impressively rich in decoration. The Great Temple at Madura (A. D. 1623) is famous for its nine gateways called "gopuras," which are covered with life-sized carved stone figures representing Hindu gods.

70

Temple of Heaven

The architecture of China has changed little through the centuries. Its outstanding feature is the curved tile roof with widely projecting eaves, often used one above another. One example is the circular Temple of Heaven at Peking, which has a triple roof of blue tile symbolizing the color of heaven.

Pagodas, built of brick and faced with bright colored tile are typical Chinese buildings. They are eight-sided towers that vary in height from three to thirteen stories and have repeated roofs with sharply upturned eaves.

71

Shinto Shrine, Nikko, Japan

The Japanese, worshippers of nature, blended their architecture with the forests, streams and waterfalls of their mountainous islands. Shrines were usually built on mountainsides or groves of trees, as were the famous Shinto shrines at Nikko. These buildings, carved, gilded, and lacquered in red, blue and black, have a setting of the majestic *cryptomeria* trees found only in Japan. The simple gateway at the entrance to the shrines, called a *torii,* is a symbol of Shintoism throughout Japan. It was originally made by placing a log horizontally over two upright tree trunks.

The curved roofs of Japanese temples and shrines are derived from those of China. First introduced by Buddhist missionaries about the 6th century, the Chinese style was blended with the architecture of Japan.

72

United States

America is a land whose heritage is a mixture of many nationalities and many ways of life. Thus, her architecture reflects various styles from different parts of the world. Before the beginning of the 20th century there were buildings in the United States representing every style of architecture developed earlier in Europe.

The obelisks of Egypt inspired the design of the Washington Monument in the nation's capital. Dedicated to George Washington, for his achievements, high principles and devotion to his country, this majestic white marble shaft, soaring 555 feet, is the tallest masonry structure in the world.

The Capitol in Washington, D. C., was modeled after St. Paul's Cathedral in London. It is Renaissance in style, with a dome of cast-iron sections painted white, topped by a statue of Freedom.

Washington Monument

Capitol Building, Washington, D. C.

Independence Hall in Philadelphia, once the Pennsylvania State House, holds the famous Liberty Bell. This historic building, where the Declaration of Independence of the United States was adopted in 1776, is one of the finest examples of Colonial architecture. Built when America was still a colony, it reflects the styles current at that time in England.

Thomas Jefferson was influenced by the architecture of ancient Rome and introduced the style in his home, "Monticello." The mansion, with its portico, pediment and dome designed with classic proportions, was a forerunner of the Roman style in America.

Independence Hall

Monticello

Pennsylvania Station

The vast Pennsylvania Station in New York City, built in 1910, covers an area of 28 acres. Like many other railroad stations, banks and office buildings constructed during the early years of the 20th century, it is based on Roman architecture.

The D'Evereux Mansion in Natchez, Mississippi, with its portico of Doric columns, is an example of the Greek style that influenced building in America from the years 1820 to about 1860. The revival was a trend that began in Europe in the 19th century, which arose out of enthusiasm for Greek art and literature.

D'Evereux Mansion

Gothic architecture appeared in the United States about 1850 in designs for large churches of many cities. Later in the century the style was so popular for university buildings that it became known as "College Gothic." The Harkness Memorial at Yale University is a beautiful tower done in the finest Gothic tradition.

Trinity Church in Boston, designed in 1887 by the noted architect, Henry Richardson, is an outstanding example of Romanesque architecture. The style was favored for commercial buildings and residences, as well as churches, until the 1900's.

Harkness Memorial

Trinity Church, Boston

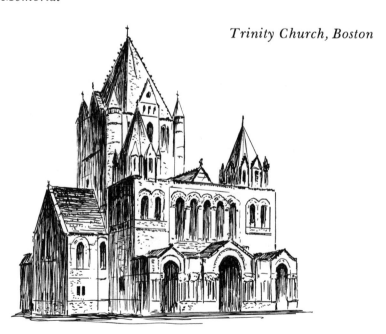

Boston Public Library

Renaissance architecture was featured at the Chicago World's Fair in 1893, and architects across the nation followed the revival. The Boston Public Library, built in 1895, is a stately version of Italian Renaissance style.

The Alamo

The Alamo at San Antonio, Texas, site of the famous battle for Texan independence in 1836, was originally a Franciscan mission. Now restored as a museum, its heavy Baroque facade and somber walls are typical of the Spanish Mission architecture of the Southwest.

Contemporary

The fast growth of cities and industry in the United States brought skyscrapers into being. With a need for maximum office space on a minimum of land, this new and typically American type of building was created. Development of steel skeleton frameworks for buildings, invention of the elevator, and knowledge of less costly methods of manufacturing glass all contributed to this new concept in building.

One of the earliest skyscrapers built of concrete over steel was the triangular, 21-story Flatiron Building in New York City, constructed in 1902 and decorated in Renaissance style. In 1913, the Woolworth Building amazed people by its awe-inspiring height of 60 stories. Its architect, Cass Gilbert, used Gothic details, feeling that it expressed the lofty reaching of Gothic cathedrals.

The use of classic styles of decoration soon gave way to *functionalism* — stressing the use of the building and its materials rather than exterior styling. Architects of skyscrapers in the 1930's concentrated on the efficiency of interior space, eliminated traditional ornament, and created buildings of plain geometric forms. Some were merely box-like; others were beautiful in their simplicity. The Empire State Building, completed in 1931, is the tallest building in the world, 102 stories high. Without elaborate decoration of any kind, its beauty lies in the effective balance of mass, fine proportion, and emphasis of vertical lines.

The trend toward functionalism and simplicity in architecture spread to Europe. Now known as the International Style, it stresses pure geometric shapes, skeleton construction, and use of large glass areas.

78

United Nations Secretariat

   The monumental United Nations Secretariat in New York, constructed
in 1950, is one of the best known buildings of the 20th century. Designed
by a group of architects who represent many countries, this shimmering
structure of blue-green glass and aluminum is a dramatic example of
the International Style of architecture.

Kaufmann House

Frank Lloyd Wright (1869-1959), one of the outstanding American architects, believed that architecture should be *organic* — the materials, function, form and surroundings of a building should be completely co-ordinated. His Kaufmann House in Bear Run, Pennsylvania, built in 1937, demonstrates this blending of structure and landscape.

Wright's Guggenheim Museum in New York City, completed in 1959, features a spiral ramp to ease circulation of visitors through its interior.

Guggenheim Museum

United States Embassy, New Delhi

Noted architect Edward Stone promoted the International Style with his design for the Museum of Modern Art in New York City. The building, completed in 1939, was one of the first of its kind in the United States. Its facade of insulated glass softly filters light into an interior which has movable walls for flexibility of exhibition areas.

Recently Mr. Stone turned away from the plainness of the International Style and brought back to modern architecture the element of decoration. His design for the United States Embassy at New Delhi employs a patterned screen wall, called a *grille,* which functions as a sunshade as well as being ornamental. Slender gold-leafed columns, 50 in all, give support to the flat, extended roof.

Museum of Modern Art

81

Yale Hockey Rink

Several leading architects have proven that functional form does not have to be rigid and box-like. Eero Saarinen, born in Finland, has been world famous for his work in the International Style. He has achieved even greater prominence by breaking tradition and creating new expressive forms. He designed the Yale Hockey Rink in 1956, a swelling, yet rhythmically curving structure with a capacity for 5,000 spectators.

Trans-World Airlines' terminal building at New York International Airport has the appearance of a gigantic piece of sculpture gracefully modeled into a symbolic representation of flight. A concrete shell structure with flowing lines, it is a dramatic departure by Saarinen from the regularity of the conventional styles.

TWA Building, International Airport

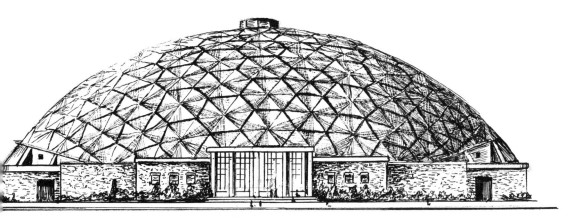

Geodesic dome

Since 1951, American architect Buckminster Fuller has been acclaimed for his remarkable "geodesic" dome, a product of much research and mathematical calculations. The dome consists of a lattice-like metal framework made up of triangular sections called *tetrahedrons,* and a covering of steel, aluminum or plastic, depending on the dome's intended use and desired permanency. Strong, yet light in weight, the domes can be constructed in comparatively short time, using a minimum of man-hours and materials. They provide a maximum of clear space, since no interior supports are necessary, and in theory, may be designed in any dimension. The aluminum-covered geodesic dome of the theater above, built in Fort Worth, Texas, is sixty-two-and-a-half feet high, 145 feet in diameter, and was erected in seven-and-a-half days.

Fuller's Union Dome at Baton Rouge, Louisiana, with a height of ten stories and an unobstructed floor space 384 feet in diameter, is used as a tank car maintenance shop. Constructed of steel panels and tubes, it is the largest clear-span dome in the world.

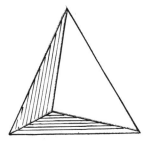

Tetrahedron

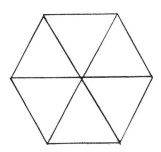

Dome section

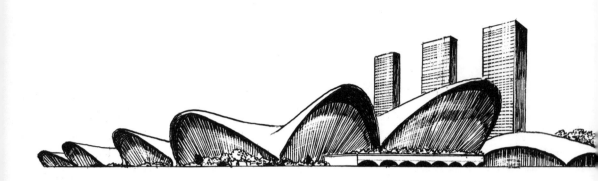

What will buildings of the future be like? Certainly there will be no quick changes, for architecture grows with the needs of the people and is a gradual development. The plain "glass box" of the International Style will probably continue to find world-wide favor as the most functional and satisfying type of structure for business and industry for a long time to come. Creative free-form designs, which are appearing here and in many countries, will undoubtedly multiply in number because they are distinctly non-traditional and have a strong appeal for many people.

Great developments lie ahead, but we should not forget the structural inventions of the past that made this future possible. The Greeks perfected the post-and-lintel system of construction; the Romans invented concrete and developed the arch and dome; and closer to our time, industrialization brought about the use of steel as a skeleton framework for buildings.

Tremendous strides have been made in the first half of the 20th century, but what further progress is to come remains to be seen. One thing is certain; the modern movement has already become an important chapter in the history of architecture.

Glossary

ABACUS—A slab, the uppermost member of a capital.

ACANTHUS—A plant whose conventionalized leaves form the lower portions of the Corinthian capital.

ARABESQUE—Surface decoration in elaborate continuations of lines, light and fanciful in character.

ARCADE—A series of arches supported on columns or piers, attached or detached from the wall.

ARCH—A structure, usually curved, made of wedge-shaped blocks, used to span an opening, supported only at the sides.

ARCHITRAVE—The lowest division of the entablature of an order; the beam which rests directly on the column.

BAPTISTERY—A building, separate from the church, containing a font for baptismal services.

BAROQUE—A term given to a style of architecture during the late Renaissance, which was characterized by elaborate carved ornament, scrolls and curves.

BASE—The lower section of a wall, pier or column when treated as a separate architectural feature; the lower part of any structure.

BATTLEMENT—A parapet or cresting consisting of alternate solid parts and open spaces surmounting the walls of ancient fortified buildings.

BUTTRESS—A projecting structure to support and give stability to a wall or building.

CAPITAL—The head or top of a column.

CLEAR-STORY—An upper part of a building which rises clear of the roofs of other parts and whose walls contain windows for lighting the interior.

COLONNADE—A series or range of columns placed at regular intervals.

COLUMN—A kind of supporting pillar, consisting of a shaft, base and capital.

CORBEL—A projection consisting of courses of stones or bricks, each extending slightly beyond the one below it.

CORNICE—The top, projecting part of the entablature.

DENTILS—Small blocks in a series, projecting like teeth.

DOME—A spherical roof, placed like an inverted cup over a circular or square apartment.

DOWEL—A rod or pin fitting into corresponding holes in connecting pieces to keep them in proper position.

DRUM—A vertical circular wall carrying a dome; one of the cylindrical blocks of which the shaft of a column is composed.

EAVES—The lower part of a roof extending beyond the face of the wall.

ENTABLATURE—The upper part of an order of architecture that rests upon the columns, consisting of an architrave, frieze and cornice.

ENTASIS—A slight swelling in the shaft of a column.

FACADE—The face or front of a building.

FLUTES—A series of vertical grooves on a column shaft.

FLYING BUTTRESS—An arch or series of arches resting against solid buttresses or piers to give added support and stability to a structure.

FRIEZE—The central space of the entablature.

FUNCTIONALISM—Stressing the use of a building and its materials rather than exterior form or design.

GEODESIC—Pertaining to a system of higher mathematics applied to dome construction, in which the tetrahedron is the basic geometric form.

GRILLE—A grating forming an openwork barrier or screen.

HYPOSTYLE—Having the roof resting upon rows of columns.

LINTEL—The horizontal beam that spans an opening.

METOPE—The square space between Doric triglyphs.

MINARET—A slender, lofty tower attached to a mosque, with balconies from which the summons to prayer is called.

MOSAIC—Surface decoration formed by small squares of stone, glass and marble set in cement.

NAOS—The statue chamber in a Greek temple, containing the image of the god.

NAVE—The main part of a church, the central hall, usually rising higher than the side aisles.

OGEE—An arch or molding made up of an S-shaped curve.

ORDER—The base, shaft and capital of a column and its entablature.

PEDIMENT—The triangular wall section above the entablature which supports the sloping roof.

PENDENTIVE—One of the triangular curved sections of vaulting that supports a dome over a rectangular room.

PIER—A mass of masonry supporting an arch or lintel; also applied to a piece of wall between two openings.

PILASTER—An upright rectangular feature, projecting from a wall and treated as a column, with capital, shaft and base.

PLAN—A diagram drawn to show the shape of a building and the arrangement of its parts on the ground.

PORTICO—A colonnade at the entrance of a building.

PYLON—The monumental gateway of an Egyptian temple.

86

RAMP—A sloping way that takes the place of stairs.

RIB—A projecting frame in a vault or arched ceiling.

ROSE WINDOW—A circular window filled with tracery.

SCREEN—A partition of iron, stone or wood, often carved.

SHAFT—The part of a column between base and capital.

SPAN—The space between supports of an arch, roof or beam.

STORY—The space between two floors.

STYLOBATE—A continuous base on which a colonnade is placed.

TETRAHEDRON—A four-sided pyramid.

TRACERY—Decorative openwork of stone with interlacing lines; used in Gothic windows.

TRANSEPT—The arm of a church, projecting at right angles to the main building.

TRIGLYPHS—Blocks with three vertical channels in the frieze of the Doric entablature.

VAULT—An arched covering of masonry over a building or opening.

VOLUTE—A spiral scroll-shaped ornament.

VOUSSOIRS—The wedge-shaped blocks forming an arch or vault.

Index

90

The Illustrator and Author

Paintings by Richard Bergere have been exhibited in the Chicago Art Institute, the Whitney Museum in New York City and museums in Philadelphia and in Dayton, Ohio. Studying both art and architecture, with degrees from Parsons, New York University and Columbia University, Mr. Bergere has been an instructor in art and interior design. Versatile as well as creative, he also does advertising work, book illustration and mural painting, and is the author-illustrator of *Contemporary Alphabets*. Although his main interest is art, he designed the architectural plans for a house in Chicago.

Thea Bergere is also an artist as well as a writer and, inspired by a collection of sketches which her husband made during summers of traveling, the two worked together to create the handsomely illustrated story of architecture, *From Stones to Skyscrapers*.

The Bergeres reside on Long Island with their small daughter. They collect antiques as a hobby, and enjoy playing their console organ for relaxation after the long hours at sketchboard and typewriter.